Popular Teaching Resources

Aboriginal Peoples

Grades **4-6**

Contents

Project Ideas

People

Investigate!

Tests, Self-Evaluation, and Answers

Guidelines for Use

This resource book contains three sections:

- Core Units
- Project Ideas
- Tests, Self-Evaluation, and Answers

Each **Core Unit** is made up of an information sheet and follow-up worksheets. You will see that in most units, "Name", "Date", and the unit topic appear in each follow-up worksheet, so that each one can stand on its own. Depending on how you structure your lessons, you may want to give your students both the fact sheet and worksheet(s) at the same time. Alternatively, you may want to give just the information sheet one day, ask your students to underline keywords or key facts, or take notes as you talk about the subject, and then give them a worksheet the next day as a quiz.

The **Project Ideas** give students the opportunity to do some independent research and then share it with the rest of the class. You may also want to adapt them to be up to date with current events.

There are two separate **Tests** which you can give to your students. Depending on whether or not you teach all the units in this book, you may want to adapt each test to suit what you've taught. You may also want to let your students use the **Self-Evaluation** sheet as a study guide.

Happy teaching!

Grades 4-6

Core Units

Migration

The first people in North America were said to have come by land, but some say they could have come by sea.

The Land Bridge Theory

One theory suggests that sea levels during the Pleistocene ice age exposed a land bridge 2000 kilometres wide between Asia and Alaska. The first to arrive across this land bridge were probably hunters following their main food sources such as the mammoth, the giant bison, and the saiga antelope.

Evidence also suggests that some of these first people migrated down the west coast of North America when massive ice sheets blocked their path on land.

The Water Travel Theory

There are also water travel theories that say that people used boats to journey across the ocean from Asia to North America. There is evidence that people had the technology to build boats for such ocean voyages.

The Push Factors and the Pull Factors

We can use two terms – "push factors" and "pull factors" – to explain why migration occurs. Push factors force people to leave one place for another whereas pull factors encourage people to move to a new place.

Migration

Fill in the blanks to complete this passage on how the first people came to North America.

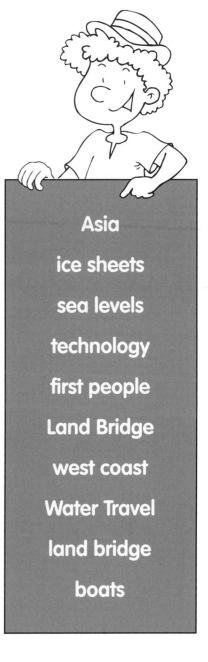

There are two main theories explaining how the 1._____ migrated to North America from 2._____ . The 3._____ Theory suggests that during the Pleistocene ice age, the 4._____ were lowered to such an extent that a 5._____ was exposed between Alaska and Asia, making land travel possible. When some of the first people reached Alaska, their paths were blocked by massive 6._____ . So they decided to travel down the 7._____ of North America.

Asia

ice sheets

sea levels

technology

first people

Land Bridge

west coast

Water Travel

land bridge

boats

The 8._____ Theory, on the other hand, suggests that people in the olden days already had the 9._____ to build 10._____ for ocean voyages. Some of these people actually journeyed across the ocean from Asia to North America by boat and then settled in the new continent.

Migration

Read the following and decide whether the people migrated because of push factors or pull factors. Write "push factor" or "pull factor".

Push factors force people to move from one place to another, while pull factors encourage people to move to a new place from an old one.

1. A group of people chased after a saiga antelope but soon lost sight of it. They pushed ahead in the hope of tracking it down. Then the weather turned bad and they had to stay put. When it was all clear, the people continued their hunting trip and they soon discovered that the new land abounded with animals such as bisons and mammoths, which were great food sources for them. So, they decided to settle in the new land.

_____

2. Living was no longer easy as there were more and more people and food became scarce. So, a man decided to find new opportunities. Together with his family and some friends, he made a boat and started to sail across the ocean. After a long voyage that lasted for weeks, they finally reached the shore. Without realizing it, they were the first people to settle in North America.

_____

3. A man had always wanted to find new opportunities so one day, he decided to explore the faraway land. With a few like-minded friends, he set off on a long journey. After months of travelling, the group came to what is known as America today and started their new lives on a new land.

_____

Migration

Imagine that you are one of the first people that arrived in North America from Asia. Write an account of why and how you came to this new land.

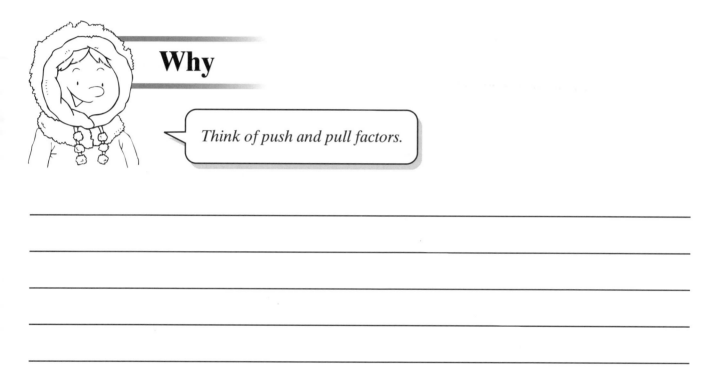

Why

Think of push and pull factors.

_____

_____

_____

_____

_____

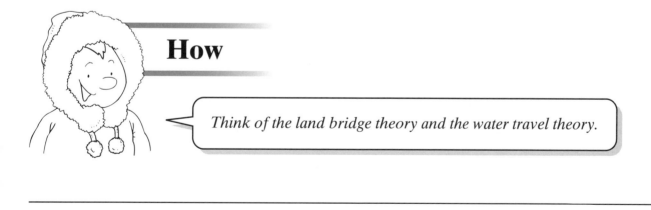

How

Think of the land bridge theory and the water travel theory.

_____

_____

_____

_____

Different Aboriginal Groups

Before the early settlers arrived in what is Canada today, there were already many Aboriginal peoples living here. They lived in different geographical regions, each with a different climate and landscape. As a result, different Aboriginal groups developed different ways of life and relied on different resources.

Groupings of Aboriginal Peoples

At the time of initial contact with Europeans like me, there were more than 80 "nations" of Aboriginal peoples. These nations have been categorized by historians into six cultural groups:

- **Northwest Coast**
- **Plateau**
- **Plains**
- **Eastern Woodlands**
- **Subarctic**
- **Arctic**

Different Terms for Aboriginal Peoples

"Aboriginal" is the term for all descendants of the original inhabitants of North America. It is defined by the Constitution Act in 1982 to refer to Indian, Inuit, and Métis peoples of Canada.

"First Nations" is the contemporary term for "Indian". "Inuit" is the term for Aboriginal peoples in the Arctic. "Métis" is the term used for people with mixed First Nations and European ancestry.

"Native" is also used to refer to all Aboriginal groups, regardless of legal, historical, and political distinctions.

Different Aboriginal Groups

Read the following descriptions about the Aboriginal peoples in Canada and fill in the blanks with the words in the box.

geographical	resources	climatic
nations	Canada	Europe	Métis
cedar	cultural	beans

Aboriginal peoples had been living in 1._____ long before settlers came from 2._____ . There were about 80 3._____ at the time, spreading all over what is Canada today. Because of geographic and 4._____ differences, different Aboriginal peoples relied on different 5._____ and so developed different ways of life. For example, Aboriginal peoples from the Eastern Woodlands used their fertile soil to grow corn, 6._____ , and squash, while those from the Northwest Coast relied on salmon from the ocean and 7._____ trees from forests. Historians broadly categorize the Aboriginal peoples into six 8._____ groups according to different 9._____ regions. In the Constitution Act of 1982, the term "Aboriginal" refers to Indian, Inuit, and 10._____ peoples of Canada.

Different Aboriginal Groups

A. Look at this map and read what Jonathan says below. Find one Aboriginal group in each region listed at the bottom.

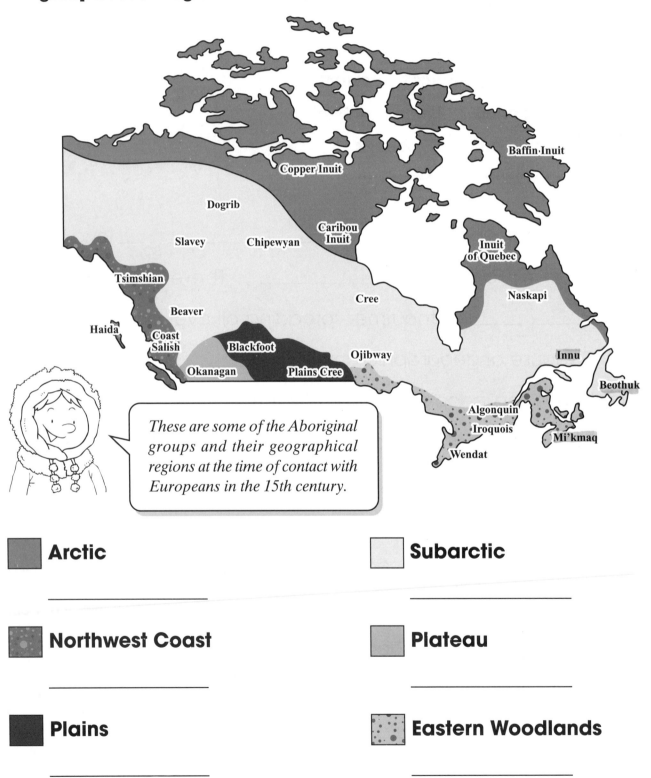

These are some of the Aboriginal groups and their geographical regions at the time of contact with Europeans in the 15th century.

◼ **Arctic**		◻ **Subarctic**	
_____		_____	
▦ **Northwest Coast**		▨ **Plateau**	
_____		_____	
◼ **Plains**		▦ **Eastern Woodlands**	
_____		_____	

B. Pretend you are a European meeting the Aboriginal peoples in the 15th century. Write the name of the geographical region for each description.

1. Some of the Aboriginal peoples on this fertile land are farmers, like the Iroquois; others are nomadic hunters, like the Algonquin. The land, rivers, and lakes provide abundant resources for both.

   _____

2. The flat grassland here is home to many herds of buffalo, the main resource of the Blackfoot and the Plains Cree.

   _____

3.

   I live in a northern region with harsh, cold winters, and short, cool summers. Survival here depends on sea animals and caribou.

   _____

4.

   I live in a coastal region with a mild climate. Cedar trees and salmon are staples of my people. Our resources come from rainforests, rivers, and the sea.

   _____

5. This region stretches from east to west. The Aboriginal peoples here hunt year round, depending largely on caribou for food and clothing. Along with fish and small mammals, they also make use of a variety of trees and plants.

   _____

6. This dry, high area of land is east of the Northwest Coast. The Aboriginal peoples here find their resources in forests and lakes.

   _____

Iroquoians and Algonquians

When Europeans first came to settle in the land, they met two big groups of Aboriginal peoples: Iroquoians and Algonquians. In each of these two big groups, there were many smaller Aboriginal bands.

Iroquoians

In the early 17th century, Iroquoians lived in the Great Lakes region, near Lake Huron, Lake Ontario, and Lake Erie. The French explorer Jacques Cartier also met Iroquoians in the St. Lawrence Valley in the mid-1500s, but they disappeared sometime in the 16th century.

There are several theories explaining why the St. Lawrence Iroquoians disappeared:

1. devastating wars with the Iroquois tribes to the South or with the Hurons to the West;
2. the impact of diseases; and
3. their migration to the northern shores of the Great Lakes.

Algonquians

The Algonquians lived mostly in the territory below Hudson Bay and between the Atlantic Ocean and the Rocky Mountains. The term "Algonquian" is used to designate a group of Indian nations with a common language. The Algonquians were among the first Aboriginal peoples to strike alliances with the French, who adopted Algonquian means of travel and terms like "canoe" and "toboggan".

Iroquoians and Algonquians

Fill in the blanks to complete this passage on the two big groups of Aboriginal peoples that pioneers from Europe came into contact with when they arrived in Canada.

1. _____ and 2. _____ were the two big

groups of Aboriginal peoples that Europeans first met. Iroquoians

lived mostly in the 3. _____ , near Lake Huron,

4. _____ , and Lake Erie, with some others living in the

St. Lawrence Valley. 5. _____ , the French explorer,

came into contact with the Iroquoians during his expedition in the

mid-1500s, but for reasons unknown, they disappeared in the

second half of the 6. _____ . Some think that their

disappearance could have been due to the devastating

7. _____ with other tribes. Others say that it might have

been due to the spread of fatal 8. _____ . There are

some who believe that they might have 9. _____

elsewhere. Algonquians concentrated mostly in the region below

10. _____ and between the 11. _____

and the 12. _____ . They allied with the French and

taught them how to travel the waterways by 13. _____

and on snow by 14. _____ .

Iroquoians and Algonquians

A. There were smaller Aboriginal bands in each of the two big groups, Iroquoians and Algonquians. Finish their names with the given words below.

Neutral	Petun	Wendat
Haudenosaunee	Abenaki	Ojibway
Algonquin	Ottawa	Nipissing

Iroquoians

N_____

A_____

O_____

O_____

A_____

N_____

W_____

P_____

H_____

Algonquians

16

B. **Read what this European says and look at the maps. Then write the correct letters to tell where the Aboriginal peoples lived.**

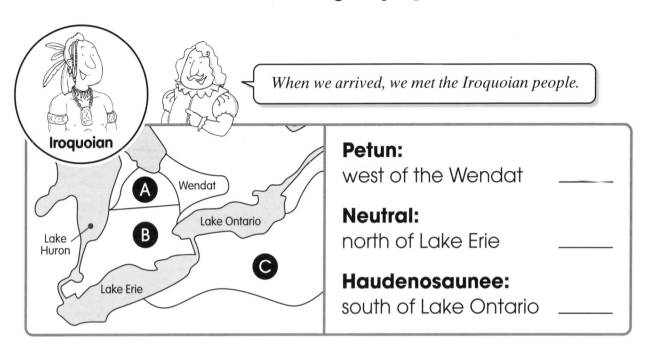

When we arrived, we met the Iroquoian people.

Iroquoian

Petun:
west of the Wendat _____

Neutral:
north of Lake Erie _____

Haudenosaunee:
south of Lake Ontario _____

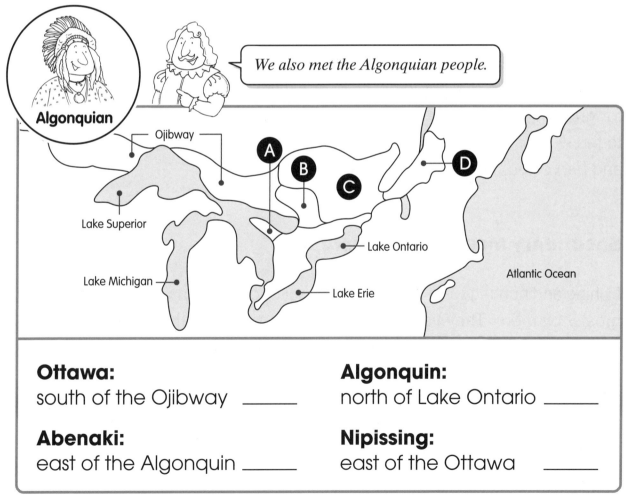

We also met the Algonquian people.

Algonquian

Ottawa:
south of the Ojibway _____

Algonquin:
north of Lake Ontario _____

Abenaki:
east of the Algonquin _____

Nipissing:
east of the Ottawa _____

How the Iroquoians Lived

Iroquoians were good farmers: they grew corn, beans, and squash, which were their staple diet. The Iroquoians called them the "Three Sisters". These vegetables were planted together in small mounds of soil. Other edible plants they grew included pumpkins and sunflowers. Growing crops was Iroquoians' primary means of subsistence.

Agriculture

The Iroquoians' agricultural techniques gave good results and enabled them to accumulate surpluses that they could consume in years of bad harvests. They also traded them with other tribes.

However, because Iroquoians did not know the importance of fertilizing the soil, their land was quickly depleted, so every 10 to 30 years, they had to clear new land for growing crops. Land clearing was usually done by men, and cultivation was left to the women, who prepared the fields in the spring, sowed seeds, tended the fields, and harvested the crops in the fall.

Secondary Means of Subsistence

Fishing and hunting were the Iroquoians' secondary means of subsistence, performed mostly by men. They fished mainly in the spring and the fall, with hunting mainly done in the fall and winter. Some Iroquoians would even abandon their villages for several weeks in the winter to go hunting inland.

How the Iroquoians Lived

Complete the chart below.

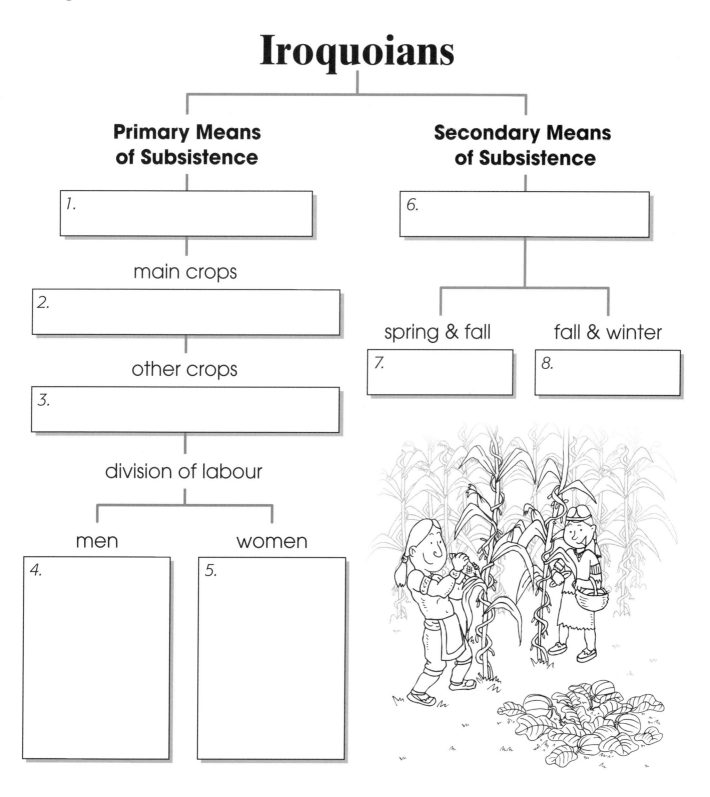

Iroquoians

Primary Means of Subsistence

1.

main crops

2.

other crops

3.

division of labour

men

4.

women

5.

Secondary Means of Subsistence

6.

spring & fall

7.

fall & winter

8.

How the Iroquoians Lived

Read the descriptions below and decide whether they are right or wrong. Check the right ones and put a cross for the wrong ones.

(1) Iroquoians grew corn, beans, and squash in the same plot of land.

(2) Iroquoians often traded their crops with other tribes.

(3) Iroquoian men had to go hunting when they had a poor harvest.

(4) Iroquoian women helped their husbands tend the fields.

(5) Iroquoians cultivated in spring, hunted in summer, and fished in fall.

(6) Pumpkins and sunflowers were grown for use as fertilizers.

(7) The "Three Sisters" formed Iroquoians' main diet.

(8) In years of famine, Iroquoians would give up farming and go hunting and fishing for food.

(9) Because Iroquoians did not know how to fertilize soil, famine would occur every 10 to 30 years.

(10) Some Iroquoians would leave their homes for weeks to go hunting.

Name: Date:

How the Iroquoians Lived

Imagine that you are an Iroquoian man or woman. Describe your way of life.

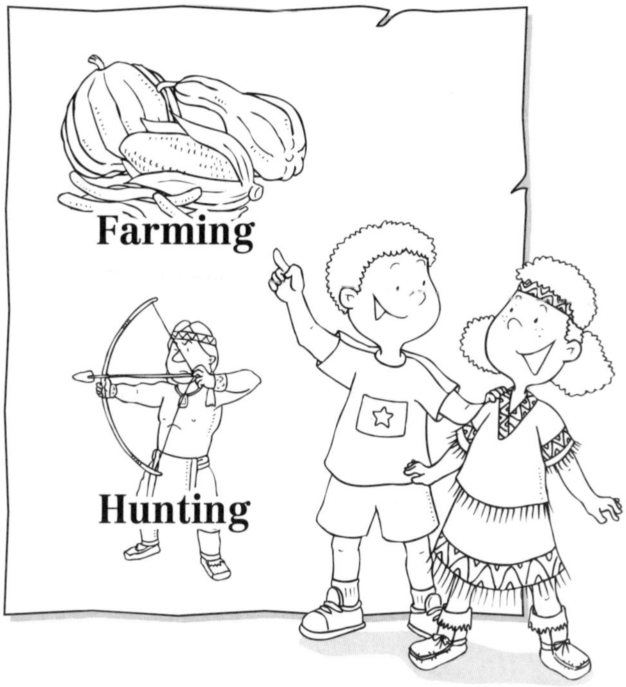
Farming
Hunting

How the Algonquians Lived

> *Algonquians like me were good hunters. We hunted many different animals including beavers, caribou, elk, and bears. We used the hides from these animals to make clothes, moccasins, and snowshoes. We also covered bent saplings with the hides of animals to make shelter.*

Hunting Tools

The Algonquians used a variety of projectile points made from flint to hunt animals. Spears, and bows and arrows were common tools. The Algonquians were good at making use of traps and snares, too. The traps and snares came in many forms and changed with the season.

The Nomadic Algonquians

Algonquians were nomadic people, often travelling long distances from season to season looking for food.

From spring to early fall, for example, they came together in coastal areas or on the shores of the main lakes and waterways to fish, hunt migratory birds, and gather wild fruits.

In late fall, Algonquians moved inland to hunting grounds. Resources in these areas were less abundant and more dispersed, so small hunting groups of 10 to 20 people were often formed.

In winter, Algonquians depended mainly on moose and caribou for survival. They supplemented their diet with smaller animals such as beavers, hares, and porcupines. They also caught fish through the ice.

Winter was usually the most difficult season. As soon as resources were depleted in an area, families packed up and headed for another region looking for food.

How the Algonquians Lived

Complete the following questions about the Algonquians.

1. How did the Algonquians make use of animal hides?

    _____

2. What tools did the Algonquians use to hunt animals?

    _____

    _____

3. Why were the Algonquians regarded as nomads?

    _____

4. Why were the Algonquians concentrated in coastal areas or on the shores of lakes and waterways from spring to early fall?

    _____

    _____

5. Why did the Algonquians have to hunt in small groups in late fall?

    _____

6. What was the Algonquians' main diet in winter?

    _____

How the Algonquians Lived

A. Look at these tools. Write the correct letters on the lines to show what they were used for.

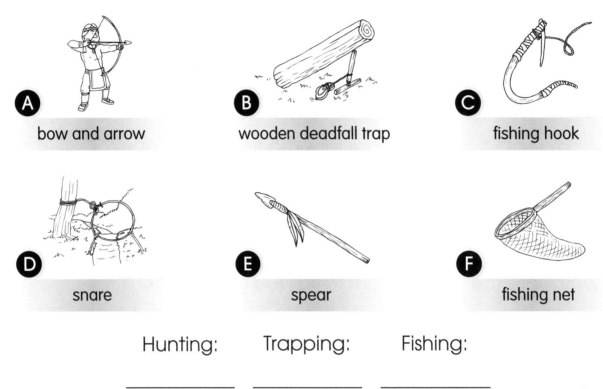

A bow and arrow

B wooden deadfall trap

C fishing hook

D snare

E spear

F fishing net

Hunting: Trapping: Fishing:

_____   _____   _____

B. Look at these animal tracks. Match them with the correct animal names to see what the Algonquians hunted and trapped.

beaver   moose   rabbit   wolf

1. _____

2. _____

3. _____

4. _____

How the Algonquians Lived

Imagine that you are an Algonquian man or woman. Describe your way of life.

Nomadic

Hunting

_____

_____

_____

_____

_____

_____

_____

_____

_____

_____

_____

_____

Houses of Iroquoians and Algonquians

Iroquoians' Longhouses

Iroquoians settled in villages made up of longhouses, each accommodating up to 10 families. When a man and a woman married, the man moved into his wife's longhouse.

There were no windows in the longhouse, but there were door openings at both ends. During the winter, these openings would be covered with animal hides. Shallow pits were dug in the centre of the house as hearths. Above the fire pit, there was a hole in the roof to let the smoke escape. Storage pits were dug inside the longhouse for storing food. They were lined with bark and grass and covered with bark mats for lids to keep out mice.

Algonquians' Wigwams

Unlike Iroquoians, who were farmers, Algonquians followed the animals as they migrated. They needed homes that were easy to build, and wigwams were their solution.

A wigwam had a curved surface to hold up against bad weather. It was usually the men who built the frame of the wigwam. They cut down tree saplings about three to five metres long and bent them into arches. They then drew a circle on the ground, between three and five metres in diameter. The bent saplings would then be placed over the drawn circle, using the taller saplings in the middle and the shorter ones on the outside. The saplings formed arches all in one direction on the circle. The next set of saplings was used to wrap around the wigwam to give the shelter support. They then tied the two sets of saplings together and covered the sides and roof with bark stripped from trees.

Houses of Iroquoians and Algonquians

Fill in the blanks to complete this description of the longhouse.

> holes   storage   light   windows   families   hides
> village   centre   bark and grass   longhouses

A typical Iroquoian 1._____ was made up of a cluster of

2._____ . Each longhouse was shared by up to 10

3._____ . Inside, it was often very dark because there were

no 4._____ . At the two ends of the house, there were door

openings but they had to be covered with animal 5._____

in winter. In the 6._____ of each longhouse were fire pits for

cooking, warmth, and 7._____ . There

were no chimneys; instead, the Iroquoians

made 8._____ on the roof

to let the smoke escape. They also dug

pits for 9._____ . They lined

these pits with 10._____ and

covered them with bark mats.

Houses of Iroquoians and Algonquians

Fill in the blanks to describe how a wigwam is built.

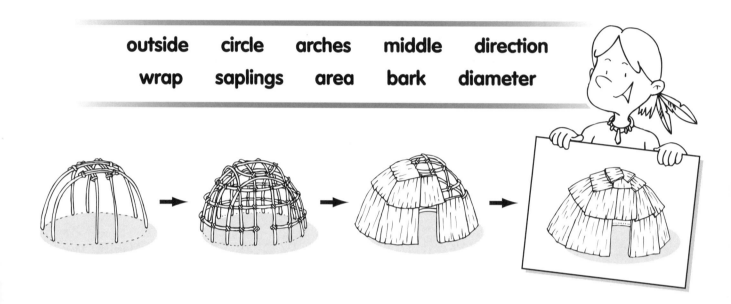

| outside | circle | arches | middle | direction |
| wrap | saplings | area | bark | diameter |

First, 1._____ of about three to five metres in length are cut down

and bent into 2._____ . Next, a 3._____ is drawn on the

ground to make the floor 4._____ of the wigwam. Usually it is

between three and five metres in 5._____ . The bent saplings

are then placed over the drawn circle, using the longer saplings in the

6._____ and the shorter ones on the 7._____ . The

saplings form arches in one 8._____ on the circle. The next set of

saplings is used to 9._____ around the wigwam to give support.

After that, the two sets of saplings are tied together. Finally, the sides

and roof are covered with 10._____ .

28   Aboriginal Peoples | G.4-6

Houses of Iroquoians and Algonquians

A.   **Imagine you live in a longhouse. Describe a day of your life there.**

_____

_____

_____

_____

_____

_____

_____

B.   **Imagine you are an Algonquian man. Describe how you construct a wigwam.**

_____

_____

_____

_____

_____

_____

_____

Aboriginal Shelters

> *Different Aboriginal groups built different shelters, depending on the type of environment in which they lived.*

Longhouse: a house with walls made of strips of birchbark and openings covered with animal skins in winter. The Iroquoians of the fertile Eastern Woodlands lived in longhouses, with families of the same clan living in the same house.

Plank House: had cladding and roofing made of cedar planks. These houses were found on the Northwest Coast where the climate was mild.

Pit House: a dwelling dug into the ground so that it would be cool in summer and warm in winter. Pit houses were found in dry plateau areas.

Tipi: a conical tent made of animal skins or birchbark; could be disassembled and reassembled quickly when a tribe decided to move and resettle. This was important to the Plains Indians who were nomadic.

Igloo: a dome-shaped dwelling constructed from blocks of ice and snow. Though igloos are usually associated with all Inuit, they were mostly built by people living in Central Arctic. Other populations of Inuit used snow to insulate their dwellings which consisted of whalebone and hides.

Dome Lodge: dome-shaped wigwams, usually as winter dwellings for the Ojibwa, Chippewa, and Salteaux, who lived in the Subarctic. The frame was made with saplings and then covered with mats and sheets of bark. A smoke hole was left in the centre of the roof.

Aboriginal Shelters

Label these Aboriginal shelters with the correct names.

1

_____

2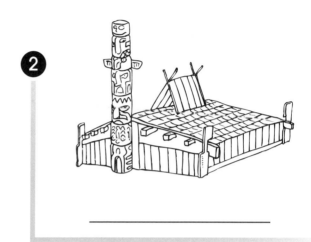

_____

3

_____

4

_____

5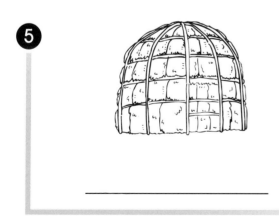

_____

6

_____

Aboriginal Shelters

Answer the following questions about the various shelters built by different Aboriginal groups.

1. What was the main difference between the longhouse and the plank house?

   _____

2. Describe a special feature of the pit house.

   _____

3. Why were tipis the best dwellings for the Plains Indians?

   _____

   _____

4. Why was the centre of the roof of the dome lodge left open?

   _____

5. What did the Inuit outside Central Arctic use to build their houses?

   _____

6. Which type of dwelling would it be if several families were living together under the same roof?

   _____

Aboriginal Shelters

A. **Read the clues and complete this crossword puzzle about Aboriginal shelters.**

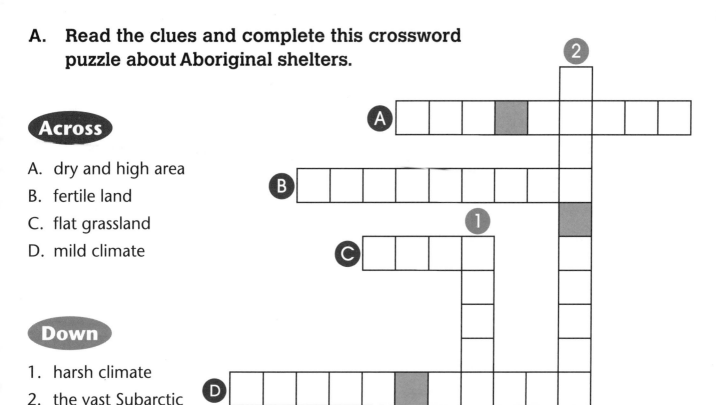

Across

A. dry and high area
B. fertile land
C. flat grassland
D. mild climate

Down

1. harsh climate
2. the vast Subarctic

B. **Read what Sam says and write a special meaning for this pole.**

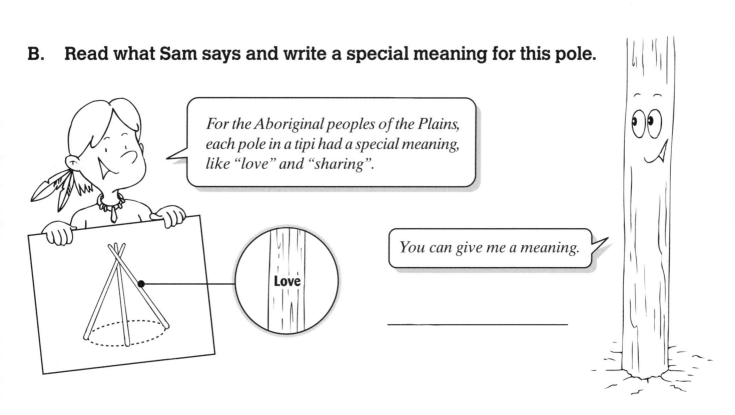

For the Aboriginal peoples of the Plains, each pole in a tipi had a special meaning, like "love" and "sharing".

Love

You can give me a meaning.

Aboriginal Clothing

Aboriginal Groups and Their Clothing

> *The clothing of Aboriginal peoples depended on climate and resources. Therefore, different Aboriginal groups made different types of clothing.*

The **Inuit** found that caribou fur provided a lot of warmth, and that boots were waterproof when made from sealskin. People of the **Northwest Coast** found the inner bark of cedar trees good for making skirts and capes. They also made waterproof hats from spruce roots. The **Plains** people hunted animals like buffalo and moose, so they made dresses, breechcloths, leggings, and moccasins with animal hide.

How to Prepare Hide out of Buffalo Skin

In order to prepare hide out of buffalo skin, Aboriginals of the Plains would scrape the skin on one side to remove fat, and then scrape the other side to remove fur. They then stretched the skin on a wooden frame, and rubbed in a liquid containing some of the buffalo's organs. Next, they soaked the skin in water for further softening. After drying, they stretched it near a fire and rubbed it some more with a smooth rock.

Aboriginal Clothing

A. Write "Inuit", "Northwest Coast", or "Plains" for each set of clothing.

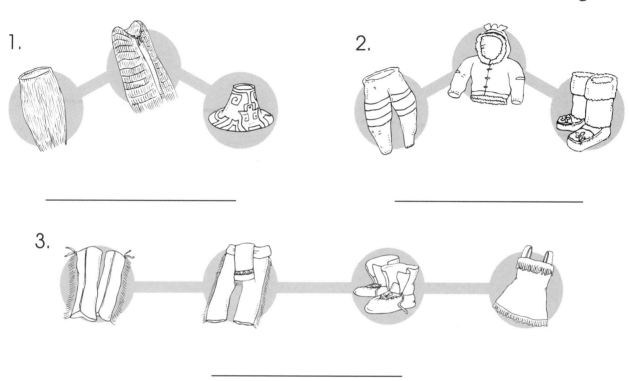

1.

_____

2.

_____

3.

_____

B. Complete the steps of preparing hide out of buffalo skin.

How to Prepare Hide out of Buffalo Skin

1. Scrape _____ .

2. Scrape _____ .

3. Stretch _____ .

4. Rub _____ .

5. Soak _____ .

6. Stretch _____ .

7. Rub _____ .

Aboriginal Clothing

Read about what Aboriginal peoples of the Eastern Woodlands wore. Then circle the correct pieces of clothing.

> *To make and repair clothing, we used things like animal skins and furs. In summer, girls and women wore dresses. Boys and men wore leggings and breechcloths. Everyone put on a pair of moccasins.*

For men:

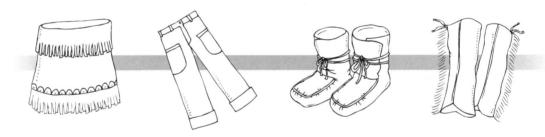

For women:

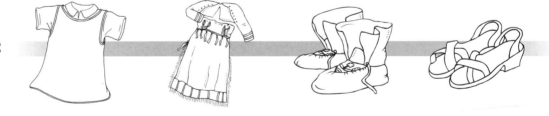

For children:

Aboriginal Clothing

A. Write "skin" or "fur" to tell what each moccasin is made with. Then draw lines to match the pairs.

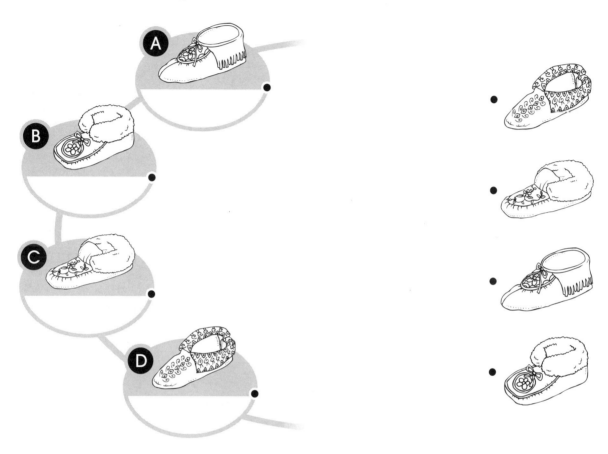

B. Read what Jenny says and see if you know what each material was used for.

> Aboriginal peoples also used many different things from the environment.

cloth

thread

needle

weaving

1. roots   _____

2. bone awls   _____

3. deer skin   _____

4. moose hair   _____

Aboriginal Transportation

Getting from one place to another was a challenge at times, but Aboriginal peoples created ingenious solutions to deal with the environment. We used various tools and means of transportation. Below are some common ones.

Canoe: the most important vehicle to go around since there are so many lakes and waterways in Canada. Cedar bark or birchbark was used to cover the frame to make a watertight canoe. Cedar bark canoes were strong and sturdy for ocean voyages while birchbark canoes were lightweight and suitable for river travels. There were also canoes made by hollowing out logs, called "dugout" canoes.

Toboggan: a traditional form of transport used by the Innu and Cree of northern Canada. It was made of bound, parallel wood slats that were bent to form a "J" shape. It was a simple but reliable vehicle in snow-bound regions.

Snowshoes: worn to keep from sinking in the snow. Many Inuit wore oval-shaped snowshoes for deep, and powdery snow, while the Iroquois wore narrower and shorter ones to manoeuvre in the wetter and shallower snow in the Eastern Woodlands.

Travois: used mostly by the Plains Indians to drag loads over land. It consisted of a platform or netting mounted on two long poles, lashed in the shape of an elongated triangle. It was sometimes fitted with a shoulder harness for more efficient dragging.

Aboriginal Transportation

A. **Match the methods of transportation with the environment.**

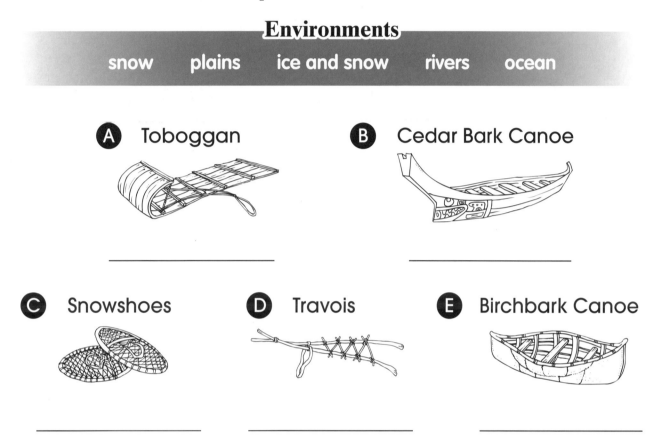

Environments

snow   plains   ice and snow   rivers   ocean

A Toboggan   **B** Cedar Bark Canoe

_____   _____

C Snowshoes   **D** Travois   **E** Birchbark Canoe

_____   _____   _____

B. **Read what David says. Then check the things that can be learned from constructing snowshoes.**

> *The construction of snowshoes taught endurance, self-confidence, and acceptance of challenges, which all helped shape the mindset of the Aboriginal peoples.*

A acceptance   B courtesy

C confidence   D endurance

Aboriginal Transportation

A. Canoes were made from hollowed-out logs or tree bark. Check the ones that are canoes.

B. Read what these children say and help them choose what they need. Write their names for the pictures.

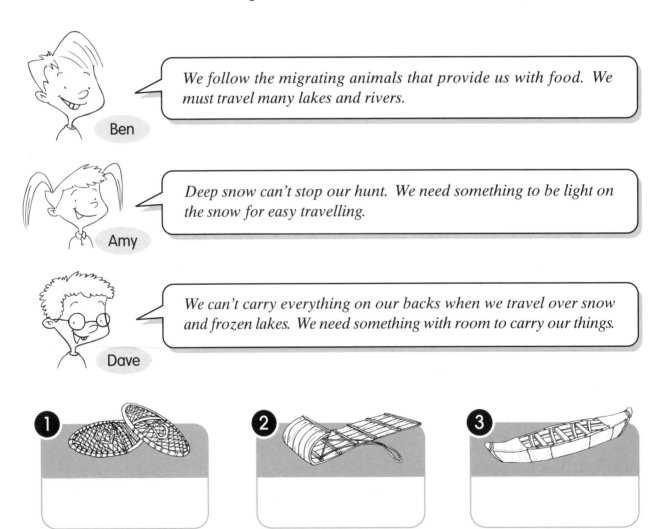

Ben

We follow the migrating animals that provide us with food. We must travel many lakes and rivers.

Amy

Deep snow can't stop our hunt. We need something to be light on the snow for easy travelling.

Dave

We can't carry everything on our backs when we travel over snow and frozen lakes. We need something with room to carry our things.

Aboriginal Transportation

Read the following. Then put the pictures in order.

How to Build a Dugout Canoe

1. Choose a suitable log.

2. Remove the bark and taper the ends.

3. Take down the bottom surface with an adze.

4. Hollow out the log with fire and an adze, and smooth out the interior with knives.

5. Place boiling water and red-hot rocks inside the dugout, and use paddles to wash the boiling water up the sides. This step is called "steaming", the final shaping of the canoe.

6. Place mats over the canoe to help contain the steam.

7. As the sides of the canoe start to spread, place thwarts or crosspieces to achieve the desired shape.

8. Allow the canoe to cool, and treat it with heated dogfish oil to help preserve it.

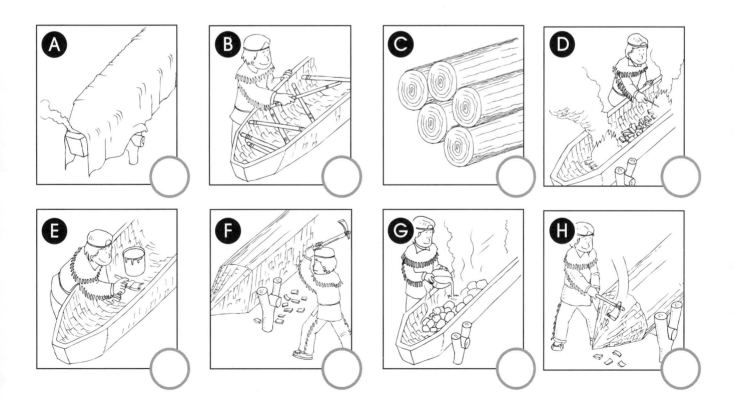

Aboriginal Food

Aboriginal peoples made good use of the land and sea to find a wide variety of healthful foods.

The farming **Iroquoians** had corn, beans, and squash as their staples. Iroquoian men also hunted and fished. They fished in spring and in fall, and hunted mainly in fall and winter.

As hunters, the **Plains** Aboriginals ate meat from bison, antelope, deer, elk, and moose. Gophers, rabbits, prairie chickens, and other small animals and birds were caught in snare traps. They also picked different kinds of berries.

The **Métis** ate food they got by hunting and fishing, such as buffalo, deer, moose, prairie chickens, rabbits, ducks, geese, and fish. They also gathered berries. Pemmican, made from dried crushed meat, was an important food because it was easy to take on hunting trips and did not go bad.

Aboriginal peoples on the **Northwest Coast** enjoyed an abundance of food sources from both land and sea. The men would hunt and fish while the women would fill their baskets with shellfish.

As there are few edible plants in the Arctic, the **Inuit** ate mostly meat they got from hunting. They ate caribou, seals, walruses, polar bears, Arctic hares, musk oxen, and fish such as Arctic char and salmon.

Aboriginal peoples often preserved meat so that it would keep throughout winter. Roots and berries were often dried to be consumed later, too.

Aboriginal Food

Read the following description about food sources of Aboriginal peoples. Fill in the blanks with the given words.

seals   berries   corn   farmers

Arctic   pemmican   preserved

snare traps   Plains Aboriginals

Northwest Coast

The ocean was the main food source for Aboriginal peoples who settled along the 1._____ . They also hunted animals and picked 2._____ . The Inuit in the 3._____ got their food mainly from hunting. The animals they ate included polar bears and 4._____ . The 5._____ relied on hunting to get their food. They also set 6._____ to catch small animals. The Iroquoians, who were good 7._____ , grew their own food. 8._____ was their staple. Iroquoians also hunted and fished to add meat and fish to their diet. 9._____ was an important food for the Métis because it would not go bad and was easy to take on hunting trips. The Aboriginal peoples often 10._____ meat so that it would keep throughout winter.

Aboriginal Food

Match the food with the descriptions. Write the correct letters.

A pemmican   **B** wild rice   **C** salmon   **D** caribou

E corn   **F** maple sugar   **G** buffalo   **H** seal

○ • tasty treat from the sugar maple tree

○ • mixture of dried meat, fat, and berries
  • nutritious food that did not go bad

○ • grown widely in the Eastern Woodlands
  • every part of this plant was put to use

○ • grew in shallow lakes and marshes
  • its harvest: reunion and celebration for the Ojibway

○ • migratory animal of the North
  • used for clothing, shelter, tools, and food

○ • animal of the plains
  • sometimes hunted in a stampede

○ • plentiful and easy to catch
  • easy to preserve for winter

○ • its blubber was used for food and fuel

Aboriginal Food

Fill in the missing letters to find some Aboriginal food sources from the sea.

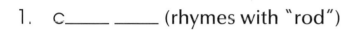

1.   c_____ _____ (rhymes with "rod")

2.   s_____ _____ _____ (rhymes with "meal")

3.   c_____ _____ _____ (rhymes with "ram")

4.   o_____ _____ _____ _____ (rhymes with "potter")

5.   s_____ _____ _____ _____ _____ (easy to preserve)

6.   o_____ _____ _____ _____ _____ (has shells)

7.   m_____ _____ _____ _____ _____ (oblong-shaped)

8.   h_____ _____ _____ b _____ _____ (a type of fish)

9.   s_____ _____ _____ _____ _____ _____ (a marine plant)

Growing and Using Corn

> *Corn was a staple for many Aboriginal groups, who usually grew it side by side with beans and squash. Together, the three vegetables were called the "Three Sisters".*

Growing Corn

The three crops actually benefit from one another. The cornstalk provides a structure for the beans to climb while the squash spreads along the ground and blocks off sunlight to prevent weeds from growing. The squash leaves also help to retain moisture in the soil, and the prickly hairs of the vine deter pests.

Some tribes grew different kinds of corn and planted them at different times in spring and early summer. That way, they not only had fresh crops all summer long, but they also raised enough for winter consumption and traded with other Aboriginal groups for fish and meat.

Using Corn

Aboriginal peoples made many things from the corn plant. The dried kernels were grounded into cornmeal. They made use of hollowed-out logs for grinding. The cornmeal was often used to make bread, called "bannock". Dried corn was also used to feed animals.

Aboriginal peoples made good use of the inedible parts of the corn plant, too. The husk, for example, was used to make masks, baskets, and mats.

Growing and Using Corn

Read the following statements about growing and using corn. Correct and rewrite the wrong ones.

1. Corn was grown together with beans and squash. Together, the three crops were called the "Three Sisters".

   _____

   _____

2. Aboriginal peoples used cornflakes to make bread.

   _____

3. Aboriginal peoples fed their animals with dried corn.

   _____

4. Corn husks were used for building.

   _____

5. Aboriginal peoples often used hollowed-out logs to store cornmeal.

   _____

   _____

6. Some Aboriginal peoples grew different kinds of corn in summer and in winter.

   _____

   _____

Growing and Using Corn

Which part of the corn plant do you think was used to make each item? Write the correct letters.

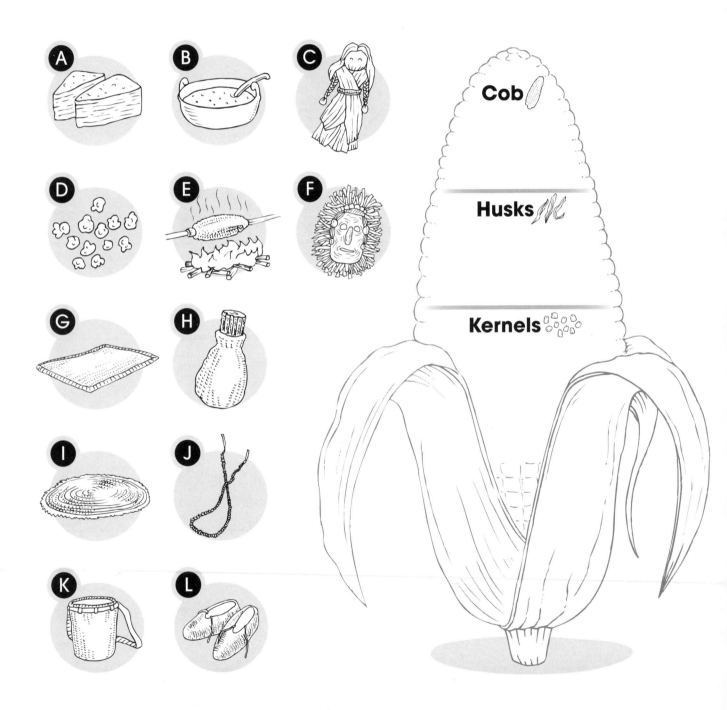

Growing and Using Corn

Circle in the word search the names of things made from corn. Then fill in the blanks with the shaded letters to finish what Miss Corn says.

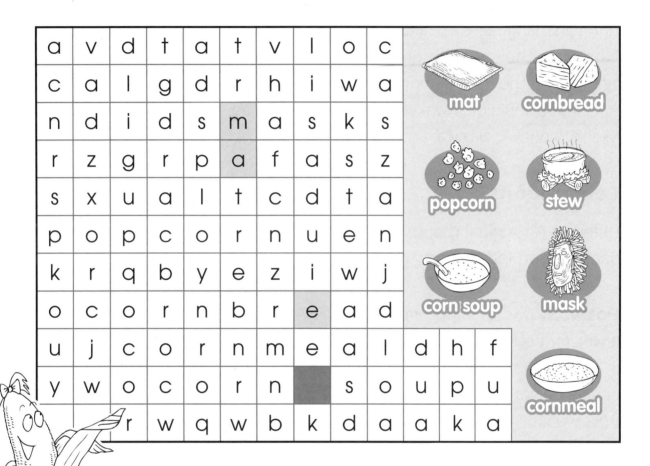

a	v	d	t	a	t	v	l	o	c
c	a	l	g	d	r	h	i	w	a
n	d	i	d	s	m	a	s	k	s
r	z	g	r	p	a	f	a	s	z
s	x	u	a	l	t	c	d	t	a
p	o	p	c	o	r	n	u	e	n
k	r	q	b	y	e	z	i	w	j
o	c	o	r	n	b	r	e	a	d
u	j	c	o	r	n	m	e	a	l	d	h	f
y	w	o	c	o	r	n		s	o	u	p	u
	r	w	q	w	b	k	d	a	a	k	a

You can also call me _____ _____iz_____ . It's another word for corn.

Aboriginal Culture

Languages

Since different Aboriginal groups spoke different languages, it is not surprising to find over 50 Aboriginal languages in Canada. In fact, many place names in the country come from Aboriginal languages. The main Aboriginal languages include Anishnabe, Inuktitut, Kwakwala, Maliseet, Mi'kmaq, Michif, Mohawk, Siksika, and Slavey.

Celebrations

Different Aboriginal groups had different celebrations, which often included music, dancing, and feasting.

Potlatch was an important part of the Aboriginal peoples on the Northwest Coast. It was for celebrating births, rites of passage, weddings, and totem raisings. It could involve a feast with music, dance, and spiritual ceremonies. Giving a potlatch enhanced your social status, since the hosts would give away presents to demonstrate their wealth.

Powwow means celebration. Traditionally, families scattered far and wide to hunt in the long winter. The powwow took place each winter when families and friends reunited to dance, drum, feast, and give thanks to the Creator.

Sun dance, usually performed in midsummer, was a time to renew friendships as well as a time for community announcements and business. Each tribe had its own rituals and ways of performing the dance, but some features were the same, like dancing, singing, praying, drumming, fasting (instead of feasting), and the experiencing of "visions".

Aboriginal Culture

Unscramble the letters to find these Canadian capital cities with Aboriginal meanings. Then finish what Polly says.

Aboriginal Meanings		**Canadian Capital Cities**
1. murky water	NGEPIWIN	_____
2. many fish	LUTIAQI	_____
3. narrowing of river	BEQUÉC TIYC	_____
4. meeting place	NOTTROO	_____
5. name of a berry that grows there	NSAKAOTOS	_____

6.

> *The name of my country, _____,*
>
> *comes from the Aboriginal word "Kanata",*
>
> *meaning "village".*

Aboriginal Culture

Complete the following chart on Aboriginal celebrations.

	Purpose	Ways to Celebrate
Powwow		
Sun Dance		
Potlatch		

Aboriginal Culture

Fill in the blanks with the given words to tell about two different Aboriginal celebrations.

Potlatch

Aboriginals of the 1._____ held

births	power	dancing
Northwest Coast		

events known as potlatches to both inform and

celebrate. Weddings, 2._____ ,

and totem raisings were all occasions for a potlatch, but it was also used

to establish territorial rights, make announcements to surrounding tribes

and proclaim the wealth and 3._____ of the host. The

invited tribes would be entertained for days with music,

4._____ , and storytelling. They were also given presents

such as food and beaver pelts.

Sun Dance

The sun dance was a 5._____

celebration for the Aboriginals of the

6._____ . After fasting, a

renewal	drumming	Plains
friendships	midsummer	

medicine man or woman would choose a tree

that would be the centre pole for the dance, which would last several

days. The ceremony, with 7._____ and singing throughout,

gave the people a feeling of uplifting 8._____ . The sun

dance was a time to renew 9._____ . It was a time for

community announcements and business as well.

Aboriginal Arts

Aboriginal artifacts could be divided into two kinds: the secular and the sacred. Secular artifacts were items used in day-to-day life, like tools and clothing. Sacred artifacts, on the other hand, were connected to special ceremonies or rituals, like medicine bundles and totem poles. Below are some examples of Aboriginal arts.

Dreamcatchers

The Ojibway Chippewa tribe is believed to be the first people to make dreamcatchers. Dreamcatchers were a few inches in diameter with a feather hanging from the webbing. They were made as charms to guard sleeping children from nightmares. The dreamcatcher would catch one's dreams, with the "bad dreams" trapped in the dreamcatcher's webbing and disappearing with the morning sun.

Art Prints and Carvings

Aboriginal peoples on the Northwest Coast, where there were abundant resources from both the sea and forest, had a unique artistic style reflected in their carvings and paintings of bears, whales, eagles, salmon, and wolves.

Totem Poles

Aboriginals of the Northwest Coast also carved on tall cedar poles. Each pole told a real-life or mythical story. Sometimes the figures carved on the poles also told a family's history, representing the family's "coat of arms".

Inuit Sculptures

Without trees in the Arctic, Inuit artists used materials found on land or from the sea along the coasts. Stone was the most common material. Animal bone and ivory were also used to make sculptures.

Aboriginal Arts

Aboriginal peoples made many works of art with resources from their environment. Later, they also made art with the things that they traded with the Europeans.

Match the resources with the works of art.

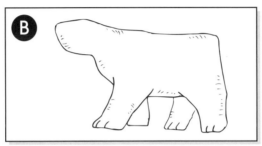

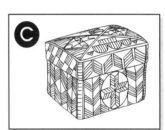

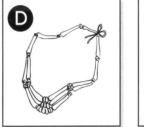

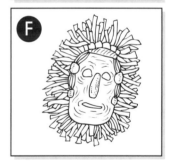

○ Aboriginal peoples of the Northwest Coast lived in forests of tall and straight cedar trees.

○ Aboriginals of the Plateau traded salmon for dentalium shells.

○ Aboriginals of the Eastern Woodlands used birch for many useful items, often making them decorative, too.

○ People of the Eastern Woodlands also used the inedible parts of the corn plant for their art.

○ Inuit of the Arctic used the ivory tusks of sea animals.

○ Porcupine provided quills for Mi'kmaq embroidery.

Aboriginal Arts

Read what Julie says about button blankets of the Northwest Coast. Then colour the designs that are button blankets.

Button blankets were ceremonial robes worn by many Aboriginal peoples of the Northwest Coast in the 19th century. Totem symbols like the raven in this design would often be made of mother-of-pearl shell buttons, which were brought over by European traders.

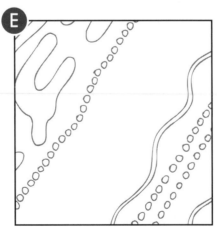

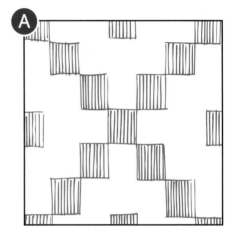

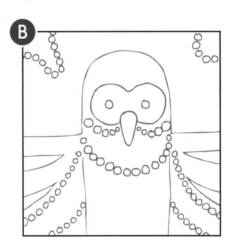

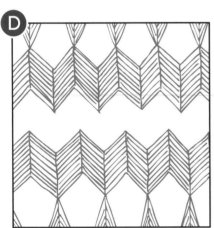

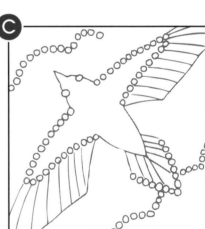

Aboriginal Arts

Find pictures of two different kinds of Aboriginal artwork. Paste them below and explain why you find them interesting.

Here are some examples to get you thinking!

Aboriginal Contributions

> *Aboriginal peoples used their rich natural resources to make food, tools, shelter, clothing, and means of transportation. Many of their inventions are still in use today. Here are some examples.*

Food and Medicine

Corn

Aboriginal peoples were the first to grow corn and use it as a staple. Now corn has become an important crop in many parts of the world. In fact, we have to thank the Aboriginal peoples for the popular snack we now enjoy so much – popcorn!

Sunflower

The sunflower was an important source of nutrients for Aboriginal peoples. Today, sunflowers are grown in many parts of the world for their seeds, which not only are a great snack food after roasting but can also be pressed for oil.

Chewing gum

Chewing gum is believed to have been invented by Aboriginal peoples. They collected the sap from spruce trees to make gum for chewing. Later, they added sugar to the gum. Now, chewing gum has become popular throughout the world.

Maple syrup

Aboriginal peoples in Eastern Canada were the first to discover the sweet sap from maple trees and make it into syrup, which they called "sinzibuckwud". They taught the early settlers how to make maple syrup, too.

Medicine

Aboriginal peoples used herbs and plants to make medicines and teas for healing diseases. They used petroleum jelly, for example, as a skin ointment. They made tea with the entire blackberry plant to cure cholera and an upset stomach.

Clothing and Eyewear

Parka

The parka – a heavy jacket with a hood, often lined with fur or fake fur – has an Inuit origin. The Inuit in the Arctic made it from caribou or seals to protect themselves from wind chill while hunting and kayaking.

Snowgoggles

Aboriginal peoples in Northern Canada made goggles from bone, ivory, and antlers to protect themselves against snow glare.

Transportation

Snowshoes

To travel over deep snow, Aboriginal peoples used spruce and rawhide thongs to make web-like shoes so that their feet would not sink into the snow.

Toboggan

Aboriginal peoples of Eastern Canada used bark and animal skins to make toboggans for hauling heavy objects over ice and snow. Today tobogganing has become a popular winter activity.

Canoe

Aboriginal peoples made different kinds of canoes for different needs. The materials used ranged from birchbark to cedar bark to dug-out logs. They were very manoeuvrable, especially along narrow waterways.

Kayak

The word "kayak" means "man's boat". The Inuit were the first people to make kayaks to fish, travel, and hunt animals such as seals and caribou. Originally, kayaks were made by stitching animal skins together and stretching them over a wooden frame. Like canoes, they were also very manoeuvrable.

Aboriginal Contributions

A quick quiz: give short answers.

1. Which Aboriginal group invented kayaks?   _____

2. What was used to make parkas?   _____

3. What was "sinzibuckwud"?   _____

4. What were snowgoggles made from?   _____

5. What kind of clothing did the Inuit make?   _____

6. What word means "man's boat"?   _____

7. What was used as a skin ointment?   _____

8. Which two kinds of bark were used to make canoes?   _____

9. What plant was used to cure cholera and an upset stomach?   _____

10. What were the two main materials for making snowshoes?   _____

11. What can sunflower seeds be made into, besides snack food?   _____

12. What did Aboriginal peoples get from spruce trees to make gum?   _____

Aboriginal Contributions

Shelly is singing about some Aboriginal inventions. Choose one example from below and learn more about it. Then write a short description about the item.

moose call

moccasins

birchbark container

sled

Contact with Europeans

The fur trade was a profitable enterprise that benefited both the Europeans that came to Canada and the Aboriginal peoples. As Aboriginal peoples did not have iron-making technology, they were eager to trade with the Europeans for goods such as metal tools and pots. In exchange, the European traders got furs.

Interaction between Aboriginal Peoples and Europeans

To the Europeans, Aboriginal peoples were both teachers and friends because they taught them how to make canoes, snowshoes, and toboggans. They also showed them the best trails and canoe routes.

Aboriginal peoples also took up jobs that the Europeans could not or did not want to do, such as mail delivery between trading posts. As the territory had not been mapped, only the Aboriginal peoples knew their way around.

In the foreign land, many Europeans would not have survived without the help from Aboriginal peoples, who often provided them with food and showed them how to cure diseases like scurvy. Aboriginal women also showed the fur traders how to live in the freezing climate by sewing mittens and leggings.

Problems as a Result of the Fur Trade

The fur trade led to many unexpected problems for the Aboriginal peoples. Because of competition created by the trade, many Aboriginal groups were at war with one another. In the 1600s, for example, the Iroquois wiped out their main rivals and became the most powerful tribe in the east.

Then as the Europeans moved across the land, they brought with them diseases that the Aboriginal peoples had no immunity to. In fact, smallpox had killed as much as 75% of the Aboriginal peoples.

Compounding the problem was the change in the Aboriginal peoples' way of life. Many of them turned to new ways of living and some became addicted to alcohol.

Contact with Europeans

Look at the following items and read what the Aboriginal chief and the European man say. Then sort the items and answer the questions at the bottom.

The Fur Trade

Items
- metal knives
- metal axe heads
- sewing needles
- knowledge of plant medicines
- knowledge of the lakes, rivers, and forests
- furs
- copper pots
- firearms
- cloth
- alcohol

1 *What Aboriginal peoples want are tools, weapons, and other manufactured goods.*

_____

_____

2 *What Europeans want are raw materials and survival skills.*

_____

_____

3 *We use a lot of the furs from the trade to make a fashionable item. Do you know what it is?*

_____

_____

Contact with Europeans

Read what the young man says. Then write the correct answers.

"Coureurs de Bois"

We're the "coureurs de bois", meaning "runners of the woods". We used to trade European goods for beaver fur from the Aboriginal peoples without approval from the French authorities, but later, the authorities set up a system that controlled the number of coureurs de bois, so we became "voyageurs" with permits. We love drinking alcohol with friends every now and then. We love life and our personality is like a free spirit! That's why we love our job so much. Though we're often exploring the woods, we also know how to use the canoe on rivers and lakes.

1. "coureurs de bois" in English: _____

2. what they gave Aboriginal peoples: _____

3. what they got from Aboriginal peoples: _____

4. the beverage they enjoyed: _____

5. their vehicle on water: _____

6. a later name for them: _____

Contact with Europeans

Read what Jonathan says. Then read about the differences between the Aboriginal and the European cultures. Think whether each difference would lead to a huge or small conflict. Write "H" or "S".

> *There were many differences between the Aboriginal and the European cultures. Conflicts inevitably arose, and the Aboriginal peoples were greatly affected after the Europeans' arrival.*

	Aboriginal	**European**	**Conflict**
Beliefs	• nature was a spirit being; all creatures had a soul	• one god	◯
Resources	• needs were met by the environment	• some needs were fulfilled by natural resources; others by manufacturing	◯
Education	• everyone learned at home	• most learned at home; some went to school	◯
Land	• no ownership; more of a stewardship	• land could be owned as "property"	◯

Project
Ideas

E. Pauline Johnson
Mohawk Poet

E. Pauline Johnson was an Aboriginal poet born on the Six Nations Iroquois Reserve near Brantford, Ontario. Her mother was an English woman and her father was a Mohawk chief. She toured the United States, Canada, and England to give dramatic readings of her work. She was proud of her Aboriginal heritage.

Learn about her life and write a short biography. Use the following to get you started:

Guiding Questions

- When was she born and how long did she live for?
- E. Pauline Johnson had an Aboriginal name. What was it?
- What are some examples of her poems?
- What did she always wear when she performed her poems?

You may use a bristol board or large piece of construction paper to paste different pieces of information. You may also make a booklet. You can illustrate your information with pictures as well.

When you have finished putting together your poster/booklet, present it to the rest of the class!

The Beothuks
Newfoundland's Extinct People

The Beothuks were the Aboriginal people of the island of Newfoundland who are unfortunately extinct. One reason is that they did not rely on the fur trade to get iron tools. Instead of meeting the European traders, which was what the nearby Mi'kmaqs did, they waited until the traders left the fishing station to scavenge for the metal tools that they wanted.

Find out what happened to the Beothuks before they were extinct and write a report. Use these key facts to get you started:

Key Facts

- In order to avoid contact with the Europeans, the Beothuks moved further inland around the middle of the 18th century.
- The climate and environment of Newfoundland do not support agriculture.
- The last known Beothuk died in St. John's in 1829.
- The last known Beothuk woman was abducted by the English settlers in St. John's.

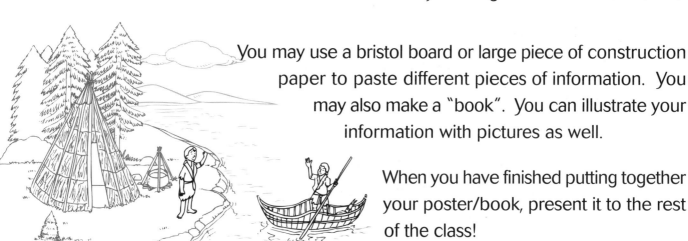

You may use a bristol board or large piece of construction paper to paste different pieces of information. You may also make a "book". You can illustrate your information with pictures as well.

When you have finished putting together your poster/book, present it to the rest of the class!

Sitting Bull
Lakota Nation Chief

When Europeans began to settle in the vast North American west in the 1800s, Aboriginal peoples across the continent suddenly faced a problem: they had to defend their territory against American and Canadian military forces. It was around this time that Sitting Bull was born. By 1868, Sitting Bull had demonstrated his leadership skills in several battles with American troops.

Find out what happened later as Sitting Bull continued to fight for his people. Use the following key facts to guide your research:

Key Facts

Sitting Bull...

- became head chief of the Lakota Nation in 1868.
- won the Battle of Rosebud against the Americans.
- eventually surrendered to the American forces.
- died in 1890.

You may use a bristol board or large piece of construction paper to paste different pieces of information. You may also make a booklet. You can illustrate your information with pictures as well.

When you have finished putting together your poster/booklet, present it to the rest of the class!

Head Smashed-in Buffalo Jump

UNESCO (United Nations Educational, Scientific, and Cultural Organization) names certain sites all over the world for their uniqueness and importance in defining our history, and Head Smashed-in Buffalo Jump is one of them.

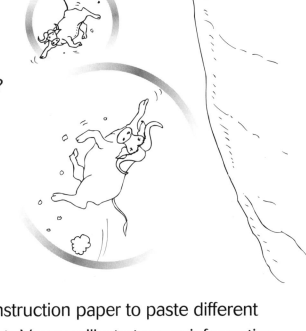

Use the **five Ws** to investigate this site:

Why is it called "Head Smashed-in Buffalo Jump"?

What are some features of this site?

Where is it?

Who were the people that used this site?

When was it in history when these people used this site?

You may use a bristol board or large piece of construction paper to paste different pieces of information. You may also make a booklet. You can illustrate your information with pictures as well.

When you have finished putting together your poster/booklet, present it to the rest of the class!

Role of the Canoe in the Fur Trade

Fur traders in early Canada depended on the canoe for transportation. We would begin our journey by packing our supplies, goods, and passengers. We would paddle for days, unpack and carry our belongings when we reached foot trails, and then repack them when we reached another waterway.

Use the **five Ws** and **"How"** to investigate the role of the canoe in the fur trade:

Who taught the fur traders how to canoe?

What was "portaging" and what were "portages"?

When would the fur traders have to unpack or repack?

Where would each journey begin and where would it end?

Why was the canoe a faster way to travel around Canada?

How many passengers would there be in a journey?

You may use a bristol board or large piece of construction paper to paste different pieces of information. You may also make a booklet. You can illustrate your information with pictures as well.

When you have finished putting together your poster/booklet, present it to the rest of the class!

Grades 4-6

Tests, Self-Evaluation, and Answers

Test One:
Different Groups of Aboriginal Peoples

A. Circle the correct answers.

1. The _____ Theory suggests that the first people migrated to North America when the sea level in the Pleistocene ice age was low enough to expose land between Asia and Alaska.

   A. Water Travel   B. Land Bridge   C. Push Factor

2. The term for all descendants of the original inhabitants of North America is "_____".

   A. Métis   B. Aboriginal   C. Inuit

3. If you descend from a mix of First Nations and European ancestries, you are _____ .

   A. European   B. Inuit   C. Métis

4. The Algonquians were mostly _____ ; the Iroquoians were mostly _____ .

   A. farmers ;   B. men ;   C. hunters ;
        hunters   women   farmers

5. Iroquoians lived in _____ while Algonquians lived in _____ .

   A. longhouses ;   B. wigwams ;   C. plank houses ;
        wigwams   longhouses   pit houses

B. Fill in the blanks with the given words.

| families | pull factor | Europeans | nomadic | Three Sisters |

1. When a man wants to migrate to a new land because he wants to explore new places, he is migrating because of a _____ .

2. Corn, beans, and squash were called the "_____".

3. The Algonquians needed shelters that were easy to build because they were _____ .

4. A longhouse could house up to ten Iroquoian _____ .

5. The Iroquoians and Algonquians were the groups of Aboriginal peoples that the _____ met upon their arrival in Canada.

C. Answer these questions in complete sentences.

1. What were the six cultural groups of Aboriginal peoples in Canada when the Europeans arrived in the 16th century?

_____

_____

2. Which cultural group were the Iroquoians and the Algonquians part of?

_____

Test Two: Way of Life

A. Circle the correct answers.

1. Longhouses were built with _____ .

    A. birchbark   B. cedar planks   C. maple trees

2. Plank houses were found on the _____ where the climate was mild.

    A. East Coast   B. Arctic Coast   C. Northwest Coast

3. The Inuit used _____ fur to make their clothing and used _____ to make their boots.

    A. buffalo ;   B. buffalo ;   C. caribou ;
        cedar bark   birchbark   sealskin

4. Aboriginals of the Plains prepared hide out of _____ skin.

    A. caribou   B. buffalo   C. reptile

5. Cedar bark canoes were good for _____ travels.

    A. river   B. short   C. ocean

6. The _____ was a tool mostly used by the Plains Aboriginals to drag heavy loads over land.

    A. travois   B. toboggan   C. snowshoe

B.   Fill in the blanks with the given words.

Arctic	sea	pemmican	potlatch	dreamcatchers	scurvy

1.   Aboriginal peoples of the Northwest Coast had resources from both the land and the _____ .

2.   There are very few edible plants in the _____ .

3.   The _____ was an important celebration for Aboriginal peoples of the Northwest Coast.

4.   A mixture of pounded dried meat, melted fat, and berries was a nutritious food called _____ .

5.   The Ojibway Chippewa tribe made _____ to protect sleeping children from nightmares.

6.   The Aboriginal peoples taught the Europeans how to cure diseases like _____ .

C.   Answer these questions in complete sentences.

1.   What were the parts of the corn plant that were eaten and/or used?

_____

2.   What was it that benefited both Aboriginal peoples and Europeans?

_____

Self-Evaluation

1. I know that the first people in North America probably came by land (Land Bridge Theory) or by boats (Water Travel Theory).

2. I can name the six different Aboriginal groups: Arctic, Subarctic, Northwest Coast, Plateau, Plains, and Eastern Woodlands.

3. I can name the two big groups of Aboriginal peoples whom the Europeans met when they first arrived in North America: the Iroquoians and the Algonquians, both from the Eastern Woodlands.

4. I can describe how the Iroquoians and the Algonquians lived.

5. I can identify the different types of Aboriginal shelters: igloo (Arctic), dome lodge (Subarctic), plank house (Northwest Coast), pit house (Plateau), tipi (Plains), and longhouse or wigwam (Eastern Woodlands).

6. I can match different types of clothing with different Aboriginal groups.

7. I can name some examples of Aboriginal transportation: canoe, snowshoes, toboggan, and travois.

8. I can describe what "pemmican" is: a mixture of pounded, dried meat, melted fat, and berries, which is nutritious and can keep very long.

9. I can identify all the parts of the corn plant that was eaten and/or used by Aboriginal peoples: cob, husks, and kernels.

10. I can name the "Three Sisters": corn, beans, and squash.

11. I can describe some celebrations: potlatch, powwow, and sun dance.

12. I can name some examples of Aboriginal arts like dreamcatchers and inventions like kayaks, and describe their purpose.

13. I can talk about the effect of the fur trade on Aboriginal peoples.

p. 7
1. first people
2. Asia
3. Land Bridge
4. sea levels
5. land bridge
6. ice sheets
7. west coast
8. Water Travel
9. technology
10. boats

p. 8
1. pull factor
2. push factor
3. pull factor

p. 11
1. Canada
2. Europe
3. nations
4. climatic
5. resources
6. beans
7. cedar
8. cultural
9. geographical
10. Métis

p. 12 (Suggested answers)
A. **Arctic:** Copper Inuit
Subarctic: Ojibway
Northwest Coast: Haida
Plateau: Okanagan
Plains: Blackfoot
Eastern Woodlands: Algonquin

p. 13
B. 1. Eastern Woodlands
2. Plains
3. Arctic
4. Northwest Coast
5. Subarctic
6. Plateau

p. 15
1. Iroquoians
2. Algonquians
3. Great Lakes region
4. Lake Ontario
5. Jacques Cartier
6. 16th century
7. wars
8. diseases
9. migrated
10. Hudson Bay
11. Atlantic Ocean
12. Rocky Mountains
13. canoe
14. toboggan

p. 16
A. **Iroquoians:** Neutral ; Wendat ; Petun ; Haudenosaunee
Algonquians: Nipissing ; Abenaki ; Ojibway ; Ottawa ; Algonquin

p. 17
B. **Petun:** A **Neutral:** B **Haudenosaunee:** C
Ottawa: A **Algonquin:** C **Abenaki:** D
Nipissing: B

p. 19
1. growing crops
2. corn, beans, squash
3. pumpkins, sunflowers
4. land clearing
5. land cultivation: preparing and tending fields, sowing seeds, harvesting
6. fishing, hunting
7. fishing
8. hunting

p. 20
1. ✔
2. ✔
3. ✗
4. ✔
5. ✗
6. ✗
7. ✔
8. ✗
9. ✗
10. ✔

p. 23
1. They made clothes, moccasins, snowshoes, and shelter.
2. They used spears, bows and arrows, and traps.
3. They travelled from season to season to look for food.
4. They had to fish, hunt migratory birds, and gather wild fruits.
5. Resources were less abundant and more dispersed.
6. Their main diet was moose and caribou.

p. 24
A. **Hunting:** A ; E **Trapping:** B ; D **Fishing:** C ; F
B. 1. beaver
2. rabbit
3. wolf
4. moose

p. 27
1. village
2. longhouses
3. families
4. windows
5. hides
6. centre
7. light
8. holes
9. storage
10. bark and grass

p. 28
1. saplings
2. arches
3. circle
4. area
5. diameter
6. middle
7. outside
8. direction
9. wrap
10. bark

p. 31
1. tipi
2. plank house
3. longhouse
4. pit house
5. dome lodge
6. igloo

p. 32
1. The longhouse was made with birchbark while the plank house was made with cedar planks.
2. It was cool in summer and warm in winter.
3. They could be disassembled and reassembled quickly when a tribe had to move.
4. It was to let smoke escape.
5. They used snow, whalebone, and hides.
6. It would be the longhouse.

p. 33
A. A. PIT HOUSE B. LONGHOUSE C. TIPI
D. PLANK HOUSE 1. IGLOO 2. DOME LODGE

p. 35
A. 1. Northwest Coast
2. Inuit
3. Plains
B. 1. Scrape on one side to remove fat.
2. Scrape on the other side to remove fur.
3. Stretch the skin on a wooden frame.
4. Rub in a liquid containing some of the buffalo's organs.
5. Soak in water to further soften and then let dry.
6. Stretch it near a fire.
7. Rub it some more with a smooth rock.

p. 36

For men:

For women:

For children:

Answers

p. 37

A.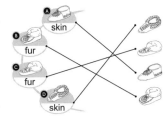

B. 1. thread   2. needle
   3. cloth   4. weaving

p. 39

A. A. ice and snow   B. ocean   C. snow
   D. plains   E. rivers
B.   A ; C ; D

p. 40

A.   A ; C ; E
B. 1. Amy   2. Dave   3. Ben

p. 41

A. 6   B. 7   C. 1   D. 4
E. 8   F. 3   G. 5   H. 2

p. 43

1. Northwest Coast   2. berries
3. Arctic   4. seals
5. Plains Aboriginals   6. snare traps
7. farmers   8. Corn
9. Pemmican   10. preserved

p. 44

F ; A ; E ; B ; D ; G ; C ; H

p. 45

1. cod   2. seal   3. clam
4. otter   5. salmon   6. oyster
7. mussel   8. halibut   9. seaweed

p. 47

2. Aboriginal peoples used cornmeal to make bread.
4. Corn husks were used to make masks, baskets, and mats.
5. Aboriginal peoples often used hollowed-out logs to grind dried kernels into cornmeal.
6. Some Aboriginal peoples grew different kinds of corn at different times in spring and early summer.

p. 48

Cob: E ; H   **Husks:** C ; F ; G ; I ; K ; L
Kernels: A ; B ; D ; J

p. 49

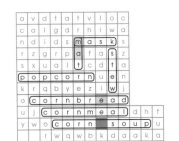 ; maize

p. 51

1. WINNIPEG   2. IQALUIT   3. QUÉBEC CITY

4. TORONTO   5. SASKATOON   6. Canada

p. 52

Powwow: to reunite families and friends ; dancing, drumming, feasting, giving thanks
Sun Dance: to renew friendships, for announcements and business ; dancing, singing, praying, drumming, fasting, experiencing "visions"
Potlatch: to celebrate births, rites of passage, weddings, totem raisings ; feasting with music and dance, spiritual ceremonies

p. 53

1. Northwest Coast   2. births
3. power   4. dancing   5. midsummer
6. Plains   7. drumming   8. renewal
9. friendships

p. 55

A ; D ; E ; F ; B ; C

p. 56

B ; C ; E

p. 60

1. Inuit   2. caribou or seal fur
3. maple syrup   4. bone, ivory, antlers
5. parka   6. kayak
7. petroleum jelly   8. birchbark, cedar bark
9. blackberry plant   10. spruce, rawhide thongs
11. oil   12. sap

p. 63

1. metal knives, metal axe heads, sewing needles, copper pots, firearms, cloth, alcohol
2. furs, knowledge of plant medicines, knowledge of the lakes, rivers, and forests
3. beaver hat

p. 64

1. runners of the woods   2. European goods
3. beaver fur   4. alcohol
5. canoe   6. voyageurs

p. 65 (Suggested answers)

H ; S ; S ; H

Test One

A. 1. B   2. B   3. C
   4. C   5. A
B. 1. pull factor   2. Three Sisters
   3. nomadic   4. families   5. Europeans
C. 1. They were the Arctic, Subarctic, Northwest Coast, Plateau, Plains, and Eastern Woodlands.
   2. They were part of the Eastern Woodlands.

Test Two

A. 1. A   2. C   3. C
   4. B   5. C   6. A
B. 1. sea   2. Arctic   3. potlatch
   4. pemmican   5. dreamcatchers 6. scurvy
C. 1. They were the kernels, cob, and husks.
   2. It was the fur trade.